How God Made the Earth

By: Raquel Borba

This book belongs to

God
Created the World and all Things.

"In the beginning **God** created the heaven and the earth." **Genesis 1:1**

The Earth was Perfect when God gave it to Man

"May you be blessed by the **Lord**,
the Maker of heaven and earth.

The highest heavens belong to the **Lord**,
but the earth he gave to mankind."
Psalm 115:15,16

God Made Us

Then **God** said, "Let us make mankind in our image, in our likeness, so that they may rule over the fish in the sea and the birds in the sky, over the farm animals and all the wild animals, and over all the creatures that move along the ground." **Genesis 1:26**

Then Man became a Living Soul

"And the **Lord God** formed man of the dust of the ground, and breathed into his nose the breath of life; and man became a living soul."
Genesis 2:7

"And the **Lord God** said, It's not good that the man should be alone: I will make him a helper who is right for him."
Genesis 2:18

Adam   Eve

Adam and Eve Disobeyed God

"The **LORD God** took the man and put him in the Garden of Eden to work it and take care of it.

And the **LORD God** commanded the man, "You are free to eat from any tree in the garden;

but you must not eat from the tree of the knowledge of good and evil, for when you eat from it you will die."

Genesis 2:15, 16, 17

The Serpent Lied to Eve

"You will not die," the serpent said to Eve.

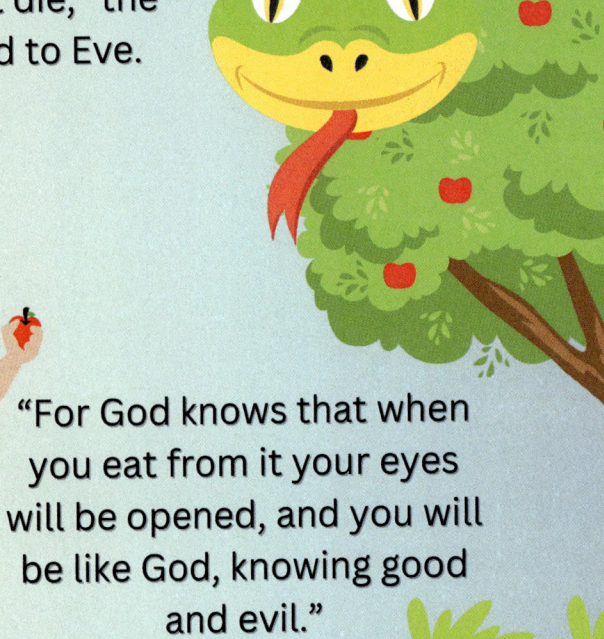

"For God knows that when you eat from it your eyes will be opened, and you will be like God, knowing good and evil."

Genesis 3:4,5

Adam and Eve could not Remain in the Garden

"So the **Lord God** punished them from the Garden of Eden to work on the ground from which he had been made out of."

Genesis 3:23

It was a Sad Day for Adam and Eve

"Therefore, just as sin came in the world through one man, and death through sin, and in this way death came to all people, because all have sinned."

Romans 5:12

God Sent His Son to Rescue us from Sin!

Mary

Joseph

Baby Jesus

"Mary. You will give birth to a son, and you are to give **Him** the name **Jesus,** because **He** will save his people from their sins."

Matthew 1:21

Jesus the Lamb of God our Perfect Sacrifice!

John

Jesus

"The next day John saw **Jesus** coming toward him and said, "Look, the Lamb of **God**, who takes away the sin of the world!"

John 1:29

"**He** committed no sin, and no deceiving was found in his mouth."

1 Peter 2:22

Jesus Died on the Cross to Save Us

"For you know that it was not with destructible things such as silver or gold that you were rescued from the empty way of life handed down to you from your descendants, but with the **Blood of Christ**, a lamb without imperfection or defect."

1 Peter 18:19

All who believe in the Son of God will have eternal life

"Then the thief said to **Jesus** remember me when you come into your kingdom."

Luke 23:42

"But here is how **God** has showed his love for us. While we were still sinners, **Christ died** for us."
"The **Blood of Christ** has made us good with **God**. So we are even more sure that **Jesus** will save us from **God**'s anger."

Romans 5:8,9

"God **loved** the world so much that he gave his **one** and **only Son,** anyone who believes in **Him** will not die but will have life forever."

John 3:16

Jesus

Thief

Thief

He is Risen!

"The angel said to the women, "Don't be afraid. I know that you are looking for **Jesus**, who was **crucified.**
He is not here! **He has risen**, just as he said he would! Come and see the place where **He** was lying."
Matthew 28:5,6

Jesus Raised from the Dead

"I am the First and the Last," says the Lord God. "I am the One who is, and who was, and who will come. I am the Mighty One."
Revelation 1:8

We can Live with Jesus forever if we Choose the Right Path

Jesus is the Way to the Father
"You can't be saved by believing in anyone else. **God** has given us no other name under heaven that will save us." **Act 4:12**

"I am the **way** and the **truth** and the **life**. No one comes to the **Father** except through me." **John 14:6**

Jesus Loves Us

"I have been crucified with Christ. I don't live any longer. Christ lives in me. My faith in the **Son** of **God** helps me to live my life in my body. He **loved** me. **He** gave himself for **me**."

Galatians 2:20

Jesus Loves All the Children!

"But **Jesus** asked the **children** to come to him. "Let the **little** children come to me," he said. "Don't keep them away. **God's** kingdom **belongs** to people like them."

Luke 18:16

"And he took them up in his arms, put his hands upon them, and **blessed** them."

Mark 10:16

How to Find the Way to God

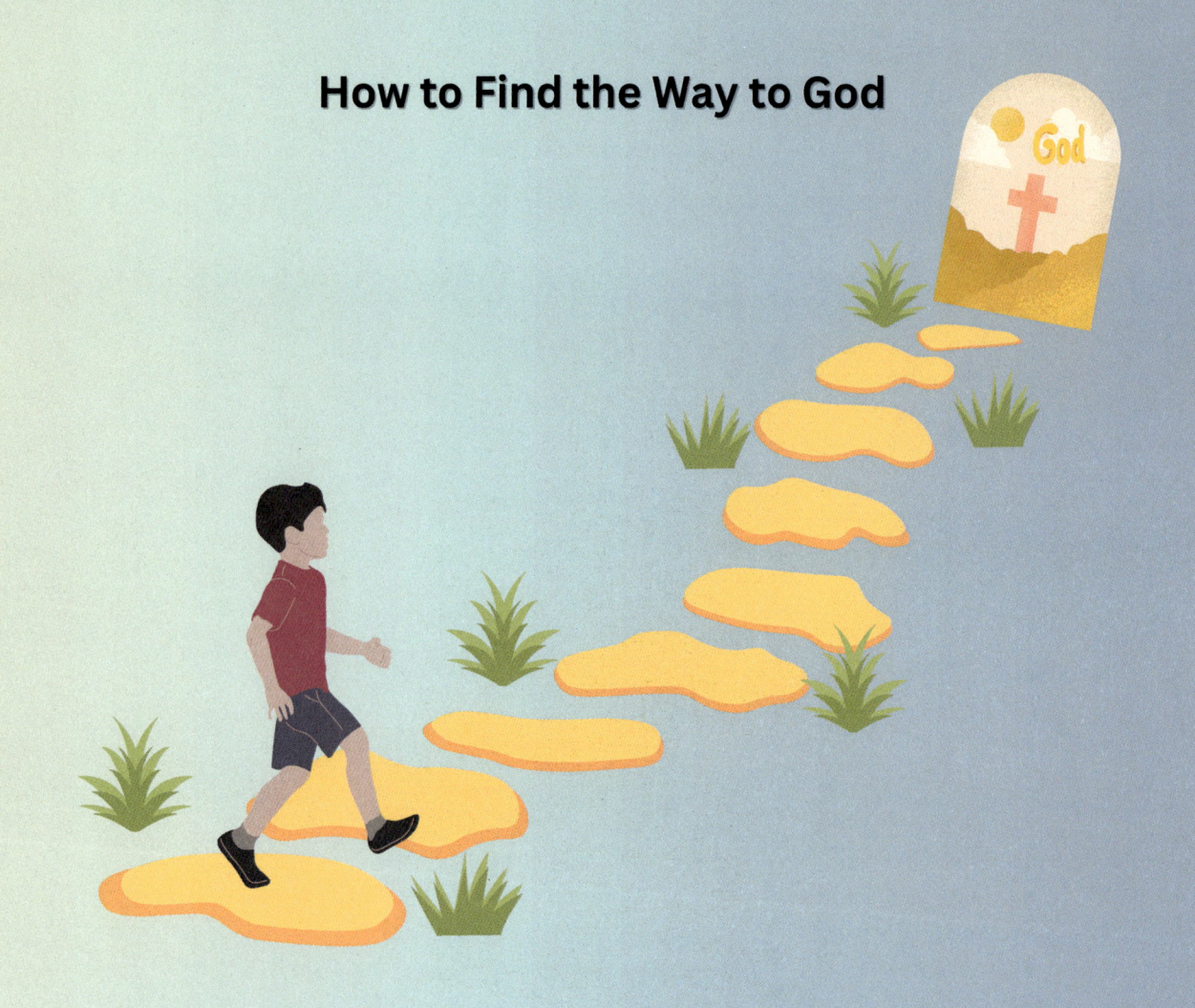

"For **everybody** has sinned, and comes short of the glory of God. **Romans 3:23**

"Everyone the **Father** gives me will come to me. I will never send away anyone who comes to me." **John 6:37**

We have to Repent of Our Sins

"If we **tell** our sins, he is **faithful** and to **forgive** us our sins, and to clean us from **all bad.**"

1 John 1:9

"So turn away from your sins. Turn to **God.** Then your sins will be **wiped** away. The time will come when the Lord will make everything new."

Acts 3:19

We have to Believe in Jesus and Confess Him for Salvation

"**Believe** in the Lord Jesus Christ, and you and your family will be **saved**."

Act 16:31

"**Say** with your mouth, "**Jesus is Lord**." **Believe** in your heart that God raised him from the dead. **Then** you will be saved."

Romans 10:9

We have to Invite Jesus in our Hearts

"Here I am! I stand at the door and knock. If any of you hears my voice and opens the door, I will come in and eat with you. And you will eat with me."

Revelation 3:20

How to Follow Jesus

Reading the bible every day
"All Scripture is inspired by God and is useful to teach us what is true and to make us realize what is wrong in our lives. It corrects us when we are wrong and teaches us to do what is right."

2 Timothy 3:16

Pray Every Day

"When that day comes, you will no longer ask me for anything. What I'm about to tell you is true. My **Father** will give you anything you ask for in my **name. John 16:23**

There is one thing we can be sure of when we come to God in prayer.

"And if we know that he hears us—whatever we ask—we know that we have what we asked of him."

1 John 5:14

The Lord's Prayer

"This is how you should pray. Our **Father** in heaven, may your name be honored. May your kingdom come. May what you want to happen be done on earth as it is done in heaven.
Give us today our daily bread.
Forgive us our sins, just as we also have forgiven those who sin against us. Keep us from falling into sin when we are tempted. Save us from the evil one."

Matthew 6:9-13

My prayer list

My Family

My Friends

"With God, all things are possible."

My prayer list

"With God, all things are possible."

Made in the USA
Las Vegas, NV
31 January 2025